SEA OF THE PATCHWORK CATS

Also by Carlton Mellick III

Satan Burger
Electric Jesus Corpse
Sunset With a Beard (stories)
Razor Wire Pubic Hair
Teeth and Tongue Landscape
The Steel Breakfast Era
The Baby Jesus Butt Plug
Fishy-fleshed
The Menstruating Mall
Ocean of Lard (with Kevin L. Donihe)
Punk Land
Sex and Death in Television Town
Sea of the Patchwork Cats
The Haunted Vagina
Cancer-cute (Avant Punk Army Exclusive)
War Slut
Sausagey Santa
Ugly Heaven
Adolf in Wonderland
Ultra Fuckers
Cybernetrix
The Egg Man
Apeshit
The Faggiest Vampire
The Cannibals of Candyland
Warrior Wolf Women of the Wasteland
The Kobold Wizard's Dildo of Enlightenment +2
Zombies and Shit
Crab Town
The Morbidly Obese Ninja
Barbarian Beast Bitches of the Badlands
Fantastic Orgy (stories)
I Knocked Up Satan's Daughter
Armadillo Fists

SEA OF THE PATCHWORK CATS

CARLTON MELLICK III

Eraserhead Press
Portland, OR

ERASERHEAD PRESS
205 NE BRYANT
PORTLAND, OR 97211

WWW.ERASERHEADPRESS.COM

ISBN: 1-936383-99-3

AUTHOR'S NOTE

I'm sitting in a bar, drinking a gose (a long lost historic German style of wheat beer, slightly soured and spiced with coriander and sea salt), wondering what the heck I would do if everyone else in the world spontaneously killed themselves for no reason at all. I would probably concentrate on drinking. A lot. I mean, what else am I going to do? Write more books? Fuck that. If I was the only person left on the face of the planet the only writing I would be doing is my name on the sidewalk with my urine.

Other than drinking, I'd definitely spend a lot of time playing video games.

What video game in particular?

Frogger.

Fuck everything that isn't Frogger.

I wrote *Sea of the Patchwork Cats* during a short writing marathon five years ago. It was during a period of time when I was writing a lot of short novellas (like Menstruating Mall, War Slut, Haunted Vagina, Sex and Death in Television Town, etc). This was probably the most dream-like plot I have written outside of Adolf in Wonderland. It's not my favorite book yet for some reason it is something of a fan favorite. I'm not sure why. I guess it's because it's the first book I've written that includes cats. If you put cats in a book it is automatically going to be good. It's a rule.

—Carlton Mellick III 10/11/2011 11:33am

for Zombi

CHAPTER ONE
Whispers of the Crippled

Everyone in the world committed suicide at the same time.

In the middle of work, people just stopped what they were doing and looked at one another. A business man didn't bother to correct some time on his watch. Three chatting mothers were suddenly silenced by their reflections within cups of coffee.

It happened everywhere. All at 11:34 a.m. pacific time. Like it was all planned. Like every human being on Earth had joined in a suicide pact to kill themselves at that specific time.

And they all did.

Every last one of them.

In the quickest possible way.

All of them except for me.

I was in a bar at the time. Zeke's. Drinking myself into a stupor as I did every Tuesday morning. I always allow myself one day a week to forget about the limits of my pension check and just drink myself sick.

I start at 8:00 in the morning. Wild Turkey shots. One after another for about an hour. At nine I'll start drinking doubles on the rocks until I'm unable to stand, which normally only takes about twenty minutes. Then I start on the hard shit. 151. If I'm feeling dehydrated I'll get a beer on the side. But it's important not to mix too much beer and alcohol. Beer waters it down. Kills its potency. I'm not paying $5 a shot for a watery buzz.

By 11:00 a.m. I am passed out on the floor. It is a good passed out. My arms wrapped around the metal legs of the bar stool, the hard tile floor cold and comforting. Zeke is the only bartender downtown who doesn't give a shit. If you get too rowdy the son of a bitch'll break your legs with an aluminum bat, but he doesn't do anything to a customer passed out on the floor of the bar at 11:30 midday. As long as you're white, that is.

I usually wake up around three and start over again, drinking until around ten at night. Though I rarely remember anything past six. I wake up on my couch or bathroom floor the next day. Not at all sure how I got home. Seattle has decent public transportation but I probably walk home, up those steep hills, vomiting on every corner. I guess it doesn't matter. As long as I wake up at home so I can drink away my hangover and go back to sleep.

Nobody ever tries to stop me from drinking this way. Don't have any family who care. Don't have coworkers or friends to intervene. I guess I should feel lucky for it too. Drinking is what saved my life. If I hadn't been incapacitated at 11:34 a.m. last Tuesday I would have killed myself like all the rest.

I might not have killed myself last Tuesday, but I tried. Lord, did I try. I remember seeing something ugly in myself, something miserable, that had always been there just waiting for me to notice. The disgust built up inside me until I just wanted to die, right then and there.

It wasn't like I hadn't thought about suicide before. I contemplated it each and every day. There's never been a more worthless son of bitch who deserved to die more than me. But I never acted on it. I never agreed with all my soul that suicide was the right thing to do. Until that moment.

I saw the empty bottle of Wild Turkey on the counter—Zeke always left out the empties to show me what a pathetic wretch of a human being I was—and I pulled myself up to the counter to get it. But my muscles went loose. Dropped to the floor. I attempted to break the bottle and use the glass to cut my jugular. But I didn't have the strength. I couldn't get it more than an inch off the floor. The bottle just tapped on the tiles weakly, like I was tapping out a catchy tune in my head rather than trying to break the bottle.

That's when I noticed it. The other people in the bar were also trying to kill themselves. But they were much less drunk than I was; they were able to break their glasses and beer bottles, and sober enough to finish the job. Zeke was the first to go. He used the lime-cutting knife. Just held it up on the bar and slammed his face into it with all his strength. It went halfway into his forehead and he flopped back. Onto his dead ass.

Then I passed out.

I woke up around three as I always did, stood right up and plopped into my barstool to order a shot and a beer. But Zeke was still dead on the floor. The other drunken regulars were lying in pools of blood.

First thing I did was take the beer from the guy seated closest to me and sat back down. I didn't care that everyone was dead. I needed a drink. Nothing pisses me off more than not having alcohol when I first wake up.

I caught a glimpse of myself in the mirror across from me. The mirror image was not familiar. My face was violent with age. Only sixty-seven, but I looked like I was in my 80s or 90s. My body withered. The wrinkles deep and long, like razor cuts. The whites of my eyes were red and yellow. A living corpse.

I didn't know why they all killed themselves. At first I thought they all got the idea from me. Or maybe they gave *me* the idea. There was probably some conversation where they all agreed that life just wasn't worth living anymore. I thought about calling the cops. The phone was just on the other side of the bar. But then I realized it might be better to just take a bottle of whiskey and go drink in the park.

Two bottles of whiskey. One for each hand. The good shit with the wax on the cap. Once I stumbled out of the bar and into the sunlight, I realized something was not quite right. A disaster. There was fire and smoke. Bodies littering the street. Cars crashed into buildings, into other cars.

It didn't seem right. There weren't any sounds of fire trucks or ambulances. It was quiet. Only the sound of flames crackling in the nearby buildings.

Things didn't really click with me right away. Things rarely ever click with me right away. I just stumbled down the sidewalk downtown, drinking whiskey and watching the catastrophe like it was on TV.

I saw an old woman hanging from a light post. Construction workers with jackhammers in their skulls. A dozen or so office workers splatted like insects along the sidewalks. Must have jump from the buildings high above.

I didn't realize it was all real until I saw a kindergarten class, probably on a field trip, lying dead in the park. They were sitting in a circle with plastic bags over their heads, tied tightly to their necks with shoe laces. The bags were filled with cigarette butts, soda cans, scraps of paper, miscellaneous garbage. Like the teachers were trying to teach them the value of a clean environment just before they decided to suffocate themselves.

The image burned itself into my brain. The children dressed up like dolls by their mothers. Pig tails, ribbons, curls, flowery dresses, buttoned shirts tucked into blue jeans, cowboy belts, furry pink backpacks. All dead. Like killing themselves was just another class project. The teachers lying in the middle of the circle to show them how it is done. The ants were already starting to get to them.

It made me want to puke. Not just because of the corpses and ants, but the whole situation. The fact that it seemed like such a happy sunny day otherwise. The fact that they looked so excited to kill themselves.

I turned around and hugged my knees, but instead of throwing up I chugged half a bottle.

CHAPTER TWO
Ugly Inside

I wandered all over town, contemplating what could have happened. There was no logical explanation. Society just decided it no longer wanted to go on.

"To hell with you," I screamed at the corpses in the street, after finishing the second whiskey bottle and smashing it against a stop sign. "To hell with all of you."

Most liquor stores were closed, so I went back to Zeke's to get more booze. I didn't need anymore, couldn't handle anymore. Any liquor I took down was just coming back up again. But that didn't matter. I had to keep drinking.

I got three more bottles from Zeke. Then pulled the fat rascist fuck of a bartender into the bathroom and used his head for a urinal. If anybody's corpse deserved pissin' on it would be old Zeke's. Or mine. The two most worthless sons of bitches I knew, and I knew plenty of sons of bitches.

I didn't want to go back to my apartment, so I just wandered the streets and drank. It was the same scenario all over town. Dead bodies. Dead rotting stinking fucking bodies.

For days, I drank myself into a stupor. It was too much to stay sober. I drank until my mind was cloudy. Slept in the parks or on the floors of corner marts. I just ate garbage. Chips, candy bars, twinkies. Anything that would settle my stomach so I could drink more.

Then I was poisoned. My body rejecting the sauce big

time and I caught a flu from sleeping out on the street one night. I dragged my stinking flesh to one of those fancy downtown hotels and somehow checked myself into a suite. Turned the heater on full blast, wrapped myself in soft clean blankets, and faded out.

Sheets filled with sweat:

I spent a couple days trying to get well. Stopped drinking. Had to go out for food, staggering like a zombie with the hotel blanket wrapped around my neck through the lobby to the gift shop. More candy bars. Stepping over dead bodies like empty beer cans.

In my sickness, I started to think about other people who might still be alive. The incapacitated. People in comas or in full body casts. People in hospitals. There were surely other people who were unable to do themselves in and survived as I did.

Only, unlike myself, they're still incapacitated. They weren't able to sober up from their comas or their injuries. They were still there, with nobody around to care for them.

My heart felt like a rock in my chest. It had been days. Too many days. While I was drinking myself into oblivion people were in hospital beds, slowly dying. It doesn't take long to die of dehydration. I killed them. I could have saved many but I chose to drink instead. I killed them.

I felt like such a horrid pile of shit. A pathetic old corpse rotting in his bed. My cries were unfamiliar to me, crusty and alien. There was no alcohol in the room to relieve the pain. I had to suffer through it. There was some cough syrup on the night stand, but I got the non-drowsy formula. Trapped under blankets with my sober thoughts.

The next morning, I went straight to the hospital district. My sickness was still clouding me but I had to see if anyone was alive.

On the way there I spotted bar after bar, open and beckoning me, but I wasn't going to get a drink. I was going to be responsible. I was going to put others first.

Some of them might still be alive, I thought. Hooked up to machines. Those machines can keep people alive all by themselves can't they? Somebody had to still be there.

There were supposed to be a bunch of hospitals all bunched together in the hospital district, but I only knew where the emergency room was. I remember a downtown street that just dead-ends right into the entrance of the emergency room, where the ambulances were always parked.

There weren't any ambulances parked out front when I got there. It looked dead. Like everywhere else. I looked up at the windows high above, wondering if anyone was alive in there. I tried to get myself to call out to the windows. To look for rooms that might have patients strapped down or plugged into walls.

"I've got to save them," I repeated over and over. "Even if they're bedridden and I have to take care of them for the rest of my life, I'm still going to save them."

My legs took two steps into the hospital, then turned me around and brought me to the nearest bar. I didn't look back. I just closed my eyes tight and frowned at the sun's warmth pressing against my lips.

I moved into a nice suburb overlooking the Puget Sound. I've always wanted to live by the water. It's a nice view. But really, I came here because the suburbs don't reek of death. Most homes were empty on this side of town. Everyone was in the city, at work or in school at 11:34 am.

Downtown is rotten. Dogs and rats are getting at the bodies. I had to get out of there, needed to lock myself away from the world. So I packed up a truck with food, liquor, and plenty of movies from the video store. I don't know how long the electricity is going to stay on but I intend to drink and watch movies for as long as humanly possible.

Maybe, once the electricity goes out, I'll try to kill myself again and join the rest of the human race.

CHAPTER THREE
Overflowing Piss Jars

It has been a week. Tomorrow is Tuesday. I am dreading Tuesday. I wonder if I'll have the uncontrollabe urge to kill myself at 11:34 a.m. again. I doubt I'll be too incapacitated for suicide if I start thinking those ugly thoughts again.

Sitting on a comfy leather chair in somebody else's living room. In front of the wall-sized television, watching Rocky and Bullwinkle cartoons on DVD.

I took down all photos of the family who previously lived here so I wouldn't have to look at them. I was wearing their flannel pajamas, eating out of their bowls, sleeping in their beds. I didn't want to know who they were. Their scents lingered in the air. In the bathroom, on the sofa, in the kitchen by the coffee machine. It was disturbing enough to smell them.

At least their corpses aren't in a back room somewhere.

I'm watching a Three Stooges movies now. They are something that made me happy a long time ago. They kind of annoy me tonight.

Eating oatmeal and oranges. Whiskey and cokes. Spitting burnt chunks over my shoulder. Pissing into pickle jars so that I don't have to get up from the chair.

It's raining something fierce outside. A thunder storm. A whole army of thunderstorms.

The lightning is getting closer, shriek-booming. I have to turn the volume up it's so loud. Like it's striking the backyard.

The electricity goes out.

Sitting in the dark now . . .

I feel for my glass and continue to drink. Watching the lightning flashes brighten the entire room through the windows. The sound of the rain is somewhat soothing. I lean back in the chair, sipping on the whiskey coke and listening to the soft drumming of the rain.

Another lightning flash brightens the outside. I see flooding. Water pooling up in the backyard. I am surrounded by a shallow lake.

The rain only gets louder as I drift into sleep. I dream of warm showers and going to the bathroom.

I awake to the sound of seagulls.

Just outside the window.

And a hangover. My brain and stomach like earthworms wriggling between my bones.

I puke into a mostly empty piss jar. Screw on the lid and toss it away.

The birds are squawking at me through the windows. I'll have to get used to them. I wanted a place overlooking the water. Maybe their presence is a good thing. A sign of life.

Yes, I am not completely alone. At least I still have the birds. Animals. Maybe I should get a dog or a cat. If the electricity is out for good I will need something to pass the time. Maybe an old dog. A bulldog. I love bulldogs. I wonder if there are any animals alive in the pet stores. Or in the zoo. Christ, how many things will die because there's no one around to take care of them? The aquarium. Maybe I should go free the octopus and the seals. Put them in the ocean. But how?

They must all be dead by now. I'm sure they're all dead. I'll try the pet stores for a new companion and let the rest of them go. If any of them are still alive. It has been a week. Some of them might be okay.

I'm not going to visit the zoo though. The animals probably won't survive outside of captivity. I wonder if the people at the zoo killed themselves by throwing themselves to the lions. Or the crocodiles. The lions might still be alive after a feeding like that. It might be possible to free them without getting mangled. Or I could at least go down there with a hunting rifle and put them out of their misery.

The sun is shining into the room. Rainstorm must have stopped during the night. Almost forgot about the rainstorm.

I hit the remote but the television doesn't turn on. I try a light. The electricity is off.

It might not be off all over town. This area could be the only neighborhood blown out. I'll have to try another suburb, drive over to the pet store at the mall and then look for signs of electricity.

I puke a few more times. Don't know how I'm going to drive anywhere with this spinning head.

Golf shirts? All Golf shirts. Looking through the closet, digging for clothes owned by the previous occupants, and wondering what the hell this guy did for a living. No working clothes. No business suits. Maybe he was retired. I put on a yellow sweatshirt. White slacks. And tennis shoes. All brand new. Never been worn.

I look like an asshole in the mirror. I put on a cocky smile and a baseball cap. Wink at myself. At least I'm the only one who has to look at me. When I open the front door, I immediately close it again. I decide it might not be the best thing to leave the house today. The front yard has been replaced by the Pacific Ocean.

CHAPTER FOUR
Escape

I open the door again. Waves are splashing against the steps. Seagulls squawk overhead. It isn't an illusion. The house is floating in the middle of the ocean. Perhaps it's a flood. It was raining hard last night, but I can't imagine sea level rising about three hundred feet. I look out of the window. There aren't any other houses out there. Just glittery ocean all the way to the horizon. I go to the back windows to find the same view behind flowery white and orange curtains. Just ocean.

I climb upstairs and step out on the balcony. The salty wind brushes against my face. There is only water in the horizon. The house is floating. There's no question about it. I'm in the middle of the ocean.

The house rocks with the water. It isn't my head spinning. The house is rocking. I puke yellow applesauce onto wormy orange kitchen tiles. Then I drink a bottle of whiskey. If it doesn't settle my stomach and nerves nothing will. I drink until the rocking becomes a comfort. Like a rocking chair.

The only explanation I can come up with is that the flood pulled me into the Puget Sound and then out to sea. How the house is floating is beyond me. Or why it wasn't ripped apart on its way through the neighborhood. Perhaps the previous owner built the house to do this. Perhaps he designed it to float on water. It doesn't make much sense why anyone would design a two story suburban home to float on water, but it makes more sense than thinking it happened by sheer coincidence.

I have plenty of supplies, enough for several weeks. I don't know how long the house will stay afloat, but I'll probably be able to live for quite a while on what I've got. Lots of liquor. Not enough liquor to drink all day every day for several weeks, but enough to keep me from panicking.

I forgot about water. There might be a few gallons of water in the pantry but that's it. I check the pantry. Two gallons. I can spread that out through a week. Maybe. It's not enough. There are juices. White grape juice. Cranberry juice. I think that will help. But I need more if I'm going to be drinking. I'd rather be dead than be without the liquor. There's water in the toilets. I can use that. Might even be some water in the water heater. It's probably in the basement . . .

The basement is beneath water level. I take the wooden steps down into the dark. Can't see anything. Some light shines through the windows, but the windows are beneath the surface and not too much gets through. I stare out of the windows into the blue. I don't see any fish out there. Maybe if I got closer.

Taking steps down into the dark until I splash onto the

cold floor. Water. It's only about a centimeter of water, but it's still water. The windows must be leaking. As I examine the windows, there doesn't seem to be any leaks. But there is still water on the floor for some reason. Maybe it's a plumbing leak. I taste it. No, it's salt water. Coming in through the tiniest crack. One drip at a time.

The house will sink. Maybe not today or tomorrow, but it will sink. I guess fresh water isn't my problem anymore. I don't have much longer to live.

It's kind of depressing. The thought of dying. I was content with killing myself last week, but now I like being alive. Things are starting to get interesting for me. Who would have thought I would be the last human being on the face of the planet? Who would have thought I would be in a big house floating in the middle of the Pacific Ocean? This is the most interesting thing to happen to me in years. Maybe the leak can be repaired . . .

I find a flashlight and take it down into the basement. The water level hasn't changed. Examining the walls, I see no holes. It must be in the corners. Some kind of leak between the wall and floor. I spend the afternoon on this. No sign of a crack. The water level isn't changing. Perhaps I can seal all the corners with something.

I spend a couple hours searching for some kind of spackle or clay. Nothing like that. There is a soaking bag of cement. I could try sealing it with that. Fuck it. I give up. I dump the bag of cement into the corners of the room. Mix it into the saltwater with my shoe a little bit. I guess it'll dry. The water really isn't leaking very quickly. Hopefully the cement doesn't widen the crack when it dries.

Fuck it. Time to drink. Best to enjoy myself while I still have the time.

The sun goes down. I sit out on the balcony to watch the stars, a bottle of rum in my lap. I only have one bottle of rum. It is sweet. I pretend to be a pirate.

I am shaking as I drink. Overwhelmed by the view of the ocean at night. Dark water splashes at the side of the house. I have always been overwhelmed by dark water. Lakes, rivers, even pools. But especially the ocean at night. It makes you feel small, insignificant, powerless. I've always been drawn to it, and hated it, for those reasons.

And now I am in the middle of it, floating in the crudest ship imaginable in the middle of the ocean. It could probably collapse into the sea at any time, leaving me alone in the great black waves.

Drifting into sleep . . .

A hard splash against the side of the house jerks me wide awake. The house hit something. Or brushed against something. I examine the black water. No rocks anywhere. Whales. I hear them. Strange muffled whale-cries, all around me. Maybe circling me. Or greeting me. Loud splashes that rock the house.

I take some more sips of rum. Not much left. Watching for them. Their calls grow faint. Must be going deeper. Away from me. Perhaps they were just investigating the house and got bored. As I chug the rest of the rum and raise my arm to toss it into the sea, a massive form explodes out of the water before me.

It isn't a whale. It's something much larger than a whale. And not exactly fish-shaped. It rolls out like a serpent in the moonlight. A long coiled snake body covered in squirming tentacles.

As it dives back into the water, I catch a better glimpse of it. They look not like tentacles, but arms. Human arms, growing out of the serpent's body like hair. But before I can be sure what it is, the creature is gone. Disappears under the water, leaving only a fowl stench behind like rancid raw chicken mixed with burnt plastic.

I'm back downstairs in the living room. In the dark. There aren't any noises coming through the windows from the sea.

I try not to think about it. It was just a whale I'm sure. Had to have been. I even heard the sounds of whales and I know them well enough from nature shows on television to know what a damn whale sounds like. Couldn't have been anything else.

Maybe it was a giant sea squid. Maybe it was some demon of the ocean. I am completely drunk and it's dark out there. There's no telling what I really saw. Better just stay inside until morning.

I go to open another bottle of liquor. Might as well just sit in the dark and drink myself to sleep. I feel around the living room carpet. My fingers aren't running into anything. Just carpeting. There should be bottles and bags of food piled all over this floor.

Picking the flashlight up from the kitchen counter where I left it, I turn it on to search the floor. The battery is almost dead. The light is just a tiny brown dot on the carpeting. Can hardly see a damn thing.

The living room is empty of bottles and bags. Can't even see the jars full of piss and puke. Must be the poor lighting. I dig through kitchen drawers and cabinets until I find candles and matches. There is enough to light up the room, but they are mostly birthday candles and probably won't last long.

I set up over a dozen, until it is bright enough to see pretty much everything. Still, all my groceries are gone. All my liquor. Maybe I moved them. Perhaps I did something with them and don't remember. I search the house. Top to bottom. Not in the kitchen, the pantry, the front room, the dining room, the bedrooms. Nowhere.

Maybe the basement . . .

I go downstairs with the fading flashlight and a candle in hand. The water level is higher than before. Much higher than before. There's nearly two feet of water now.

Christ, what happened? It wasn't leaking like this before. The cement was holding it together pretty good last time I looked. I don't think the house will last until morning.

CHAPTER FIVE
Secret Places

Forget the liquor. I've got to start thinking of ways to survive. A raft. I can build a raft out of the furniture. How the hell do you build a raft? Might as well try to do something. Maybe a bed will float. I've seen a mattress float on water before. Maybe they have an air mattress.

I take a few candles, hot wax dripping down my knuckles, and go upstairs to the master bedroom. The room is soaked. Was it raining in here? I didn't notice any wetness before. It is coming from the bed. A water bed?

Setting candles up on the night stand, I tear the wet sheet from the mattress. But, it's not a mattress. It seems to be more like a block of ice. I touch it. Freezing. It *is* ice.

When did this ice get here? I must be going out of my mind. There's no possible way this ice could have been here before. The owners of this house have been dead for a week.

I examine the ice closer. There is something frozen inside. A woman. The ice is cloudy. Hard to make any features out. Just a female body. Breasts. That's about all. I also see the frame of the bed is some kind of cooling system. When the electricity went out it probably started melting. There are cables connected to the night stands and the dresser. I follow the cables. The dresser isn't really a dresser. It is some kind of control panel disguised as a dresser.

What in the hell is this?

I go to the next room and open the bed. It is just a bed. But the dresser contains other frozen specimens. Fish. Turtle-like creatures. Can't really tell what they are. Who the hell used to live in this house?

I go through other rooms. Behind all the furniture is hidden equipment, like this house was one of those secret UFO labs from the TV. But why? Why put a secret lab in the middle of a suburb? Why make it capable of floating on the ocean?

I pick up some of the photos that were hanging on the walls. To see who the hell used to live here. The people in the pictures have bright plastic smiles. I open one of the frames and pull out the picture. It was cut out of a clothing magazine. The other photos were also cut from magazines. Some of them are the pictures that came with the frames. They all look like they are part of the same family, but they are all different people from different families. It is all a fake, a cover. For some reason, the people who used to live here wanted to disguise this house as a regular house.

The living room and kitchen are real. The person who owned this place must have cooked here, watched television here, but I don't think they actually lived here. There might even be some secret rooms I don't know about.

The garage. I haven't been in the garage yet. I know this house has one. I saw it on the way in. But I don't see any door that leads to it. There's got to be a way in.

I examine the walls for secret passages. My buzz

fading and headache beginning to pound, but I've got to investigate. It's easy to figure out where the garage is. It is on the other side of the dinning room wall. But where is the door?

The pantry. It might not have been a pantry originally. Maybe a laundry room with an entrance to the garage. They turned it into a pantry to disguise the garage door. Why go through such trouble?

There is a doorknob behind some Fruit Loops. Just as I thought. When the door opens, the shelves open with it. Most of the food on the shelves has been fastened to the wood so they won't fall every time somebody opens the door. Inside, it doesn't look like a garage at all.

I need several candles to brighten the room. So much stuff casting shadows. So much equipment. It definitely is some kind of laboratory. Not any kind of laboratory I've ever seen. No microscopes or test tubes with multi-colored liquids. Not even a bunch of computers. It's more alien. Coils of steel and smooth beetle-shell devices. It definitely looks alien to me.

The garage is a self-contained room. The walls, ceiling, and floor are all a hard plastic material. Like the garage was built around this room. Like the whole house was built around this room. The outside garage door doesn't really open. For all I know, the insides of all the houses in the neighborhood might have looked like this.

Whoever used to live here is dead now. Whether they were some kind of independent scientists advanced far beyond our government's understanding or some kind of alien race living among our people, they are dead. Just like everyone else, they killed themselves. There are several more blocks of ice like the one upstairs. All of them contain women, frozen inside. Water all over the floor.

This is fucked up. Where the hell did all these women come from? Are they alive? It sure doesn't look like it. They look like stiffs frozen in ice. Wait a minute . . .

My alcohol is missing. My food is missing. Somebody could be here with me. Hiding from me. It is a big dark house. Someone could be hiding anywhere.

I go back in the house. Upstairs. There isn't any kind of weapon in the house. No baseball bats. No golf clubs. There are stone bookends on one of the dressers. No books. Just the book ends. I figure if there is someone else in the house I can throw these at them. Assuming the other person isn't armed. He has been hiding from me so I assume he is unarmed. And easily intimidated.

After searching the house top to bottom three times, I realize there's no way anyone else could be in here with me. Unless there is another secret room around here. Unless the house is haunted.

I keep searching, looking for another secret door. But there's nothing. Nothing like the garage. In one of the upstairs bedrooms there isn't a closet to be seen, but enough space for a closet. No possible door hidden anywhere, thigh. Unless . . .

The balcony. You might have to go out on the balcony to get into the secret closet room. The door could be disguised in the bricks.

Forget the secret door. I see a light up ahead. A yellow light. A ship? A town on an island maybe? Some kind

31

of lighthouse? Maybe some other old fool drifting in a stray house in the middle of the ocean? How the hell did that bastard get his electricity going? Whatever it is, I'm drifting right for it.

I drift closer to the light. It looks like people sitting in the water up there. The closer I get, the more they look like people. Some kind of gigantic sculpture of two naked women sitting back to back, their heads and hips conjoined, stretching probably two hundred feet out of the water. It's very strange to see a large sculpture in the middle of the ocean, but at least it is some kind of sign of life. Perhaps there is a civilized island nearby.

But there aren't any lights beyond the sculpture. There isn't any sign of land at all. Just this large structure of two conjoined twins with lights freckling their bodies.

Drifting closer . . .

What the hell is that thing?

It's not a sculpture. It's some kind of building. Those lights are coming from windows. A house. Does somebody live way out here, in the middle of the sea? There isn't a dock. No sign of ships. If somebody lives here they wouldn't be able to come and go by boat. I'm not imagining this. There really is some kind of women-shaped house in the sea up ahead . . .

CHAPTER SIX
Nerve Works

I don't care who lives there. This house is sinking and that's the only place I have to go. The owner will just have to accept me. That is, if he didn't already kill himself.

I go down into the basement to look for a rope. The water level is higher. Much higher. Most of the basement is underwater. This ship is sinking fast. I might have to swim out of here.

There isn't any rope but there is a chain hanging from a rafter on the other side of the room. A long, heavy chain with an anchor on the end of it. An anchor? What the hell does a house need with an anchor? The owner had to have made this house floatable on purpose. Too bad he didn't do a better job.

The basement water is icy cold when I plunge inside. My breaths become hyper-piercing and my muscles tighten up. In a snap I'm sober, with heightened senses, as usual. I fucking hate the effects of cold water. When I pull the chain from the rafters, I realize how heavy it is. It doesn't seem hefty enough to weigh down a house/ship this size. Seems more like an anchor for a dinghy. But still, heavy as hell.

The anchor gets caught on every stupid step on the way up the stairs, but I get it out of the basement. Shivering, teeth chattering as I open the front door. The women-shaped building is closing in. Green millipede vines grow up the women's arms. Flowers grow from a crotch. A garden. Somebody has to live here.

"Hello," I call out.

Many of the windows are lit but there are no signs of movement within. No people.

"Hello up there."

No answer.

The wind blows the ship away from the house. I'm going to go past it.

"Shit," I grumble, examining the house for a place to tie the anchor.

"I'm coming aboard," I call out again.

I open the window to my right, then weave the anchor out through the doorway and in through the window, and wrap it around a few more times. After tangling the chain around the anchor, it should be able to hold steady.

"Hopefully this isn't a hallucination," I say, teeth-chattering at myself.

Then I dive into the cold black water.

It's a bit farther than I thought it was. My lungs stabbing with quick breaths. Why is it always so hard to breathe when I'm in cold water? I nearly hyperventilate. And these damn ugly golf clothes I'm wearing are so heavy and hard to swim in.

I only have one side of the chain, the rest still in the

house. Hopefully the chain will unravel with me or I'll have a difficult swim. I'm already having a difficult swim.

Splashing through the dark liquid, all I can think about is that weird serpent creature I saw in the ocean earlier. I can't stop imagining it is just below me, looking up at me, its human arms/tentacles waving at me. Bubbles foam out of the water as I swim. It seems like dozens of creatures are lurking in the black water below, but I can't turn back. I keep swimming. Praying.

I make it there before anything grabs my feet. The water stops bubbling. I scrape my armpits and belly against the concrete while trying to lift myself out of the water onto the steps leading up to the doorway. A gust of wind freezes my wet clothes, curls my spine.

I wrap the chain around one of the big toes of the building. Coiling the chain up, trying to reel the house in. Most of the chain is under the water somewhere.

Before I tighten up the slack, the chain under the surface catches on something. Stuck. Not sure what it is, but the chain won't budge. I try shaking it, jerking it side to side, in a loop, but nothing frees it.

Maybe I should check out the building first and try again later. Maybe there's somebody who can help me.

Above the door of the building there is a sign that reads:

NERVE WORKS

What the hell does that mean? Nerve Works. Is it the name of this structure? Maybe it's the name of the company that built this structure.

I knock on the door.

There isn't a doorbell.

The wind freezes my wet back. My gooseflesh is getting gooseflesh.

I knock again.

"Hello?" I call out, teeth chattering.

Knock. Knock. Knock.

"Is anybody in there?"

Nothing. No answer. No sounds at all coming from within.

I try the doorknob. It isn't locked. There isn't any lock on the door at all.

I open it. It doesn't creak. It seems brand new.

It is a mansion inside. Vast. Empty. Just black and white checkered tiles that stretch a hundred yards or so. Hanging from the ceiling is an electric chandelier that brightens the room.

Electricity?

It is the only light source in the room. The distance is dim.

"Hello?" I call out.

Maybe the occupants are asleep. It is probably late.

"Sorry to disturb you, but I've been stranded on your doorstep."

My teeth aren't chattering anymore. It is warmer inside. The house has heat.

No one answers.

Perhaps they can't hear me.

Maybe they are upstairs.

The checkered tiles continue up a large spiral staircase that leads into shadows.

I approach the stairs. My squishy footsteps echo through the empty space.

"Hello?" I call up from the bottom of the staircase.

It is dark up there.

I take some steps.

"Is anybody here?" My voice echoes loudly, but still no response.

I walk up the stairs and peer into the next floor.

It is a dark hallway that stretches in both directions, lined with dozens of doors. There is only one light near the end of the hall. About seven doors down, in the darkness, there is a dim light shining out from a crack under a door.

Somebody must be in there.

I don't hear any sounds at all, but there is a light.

"Hello?" I call out, taking a few steps into the hallway.

A crashing noise.

I fall backwards, nearly down the staircase, but I catch myself on the wooden railing. It came from outside. I look back, squatting down to see through the entrance. The floating house has crashed into the side of the Nerve Works. Candlelight is still flickering from within.

I turn away from it. Back to the hallway.

The light is no longer there. Whoever was in the room must have turned it off.

"Hello?" I call out. "I'm not dangerous. I'm stranded here. I need help."

No response.

I search for a light switch. The walls are blank. No switches, no buttons. Nothing. Just white.

I go back down the stairs to the floating house. It's not going to be here for long. I better collect supplies while I still can. Don't know how stocked this place is. Luckily the house crashed door-first. I'm able to walk right inside. But the house is slanted upward a bit, making it difficult on my spine as I walk up the slope, nearly tripping over the anchor chain.

I go straight for the kitchen. Get green garbage bags out from below the sink and start filling them. I start with the pantry, taking everything. Ripping apart the boxes glued to the shelves. Just dumping it all in the bags. Not worried about what I can use and what I can't.

The bags break all over the floor of the Nerve Works when I bring them in. It's okay. I go in for more. Fill every garbage bag there is and take them in.

But what I really want is some kind of weapon. I'd feel safer with a weapon. There aren't any knives in the kitchen. Forks and butter knives. Don't know what the hell I'll do with forks and butter knives. Maybe there's something in the lab.

Nothing in the lab either. Just a bunch of junk. The candles in here are still burning strong. If I knew what the fuck all of this lab equipment actually did I might have a use for it, but with my lack of technical knowledge it all might as well be just a bunch of empty milk cartons.

There is something moving in the corner. I take a candle and step closer. It's coming from the blocks of ice. One of them has melted enough to expose a hand of one of the frozen bodies. And the fingers on the hand are moving. I go to it. The hand is covered in tattoos. I touch the palm and the fingers curl around me.

Is she alive?

Her hand lets go and begins to move, making some kind of hand signals, like she is conscious and trying to communicate with me.

She is still alive.

All of them are alive.

I've got to get them out of here.

I try melting the ice with the candle flame. Not fast enough. I've got to get the blocks of ice out of here and find a way to melt them later.

I just grab the ice from the back and pull. The cold bites at my flesh with needle teeth, but I put up with the pain. I slam the ice out of its cooling mechanism and drag it out of the lab.

Water fills the house. Just a few more inches, but it comes fast. I need to get them all out quickly. There's probably a dozen women here. All still alive.

The downward slope helps a lot. I push the block of ice out of the doorway and up the steps to the Nerve Works. The girl's fingers flapping at me.

I turn around and go for the next one. Running. Need to get them out faster. The second one I throw out of the freezing mechanism and push it out of the house in only a few minutes. Adrenalin must have taken over me.

I do it again. I rip a block of ice out of the wall, but it crashes against the garage floor. It cracks. I pull on the block of ice and the crack widens, splits the ice into halves. Blood fills the saltwater floor.

"Shit!" I cry, punching myself in the face.

I see the girl's insides slip out of her open halves. Their flesh isn't frozen. Only the ice that contains them. How is this possible? How do they breathe?

I go for the next block of ice: a black form stares at me inside. I'll be a little more careful this time, gently taking her out of the wall and pulling her across the floor.

It's taking too long, though. The water is getting deep. The house is slipping down into the sea. I have to push the block uphill to the entrance. Push it up out of the door. But it misses the steps of the Nerve Works and plunges into the sea.

I slam my head into the walls.
Stupid. Stupid. Asshole.

Have to keep trying. There are still so many left in here, but I'll be lucky to get just one more.

Upstairs.

This one might be easier. The one disguised as a bed in the master bedroom. There's no water up here. The stairs are at a good slant. My hands are frozen. They feel like I'm wearing gloves. Underneath the gloves, my flesh feels raw. Gummy.

I go around to the other side of the bed and flip the ice block up like a mattress. It might be easier to think of it as a mattress. I'm just helping a friend move, just loading this mattress into his truck.

I push it out of the master bedroom and into the hall, go down the stairs, still sloped slightly downward. We splash into the water. It's deep now. Very deep. Up to my shoulders.

The block of ice pops out of my grip and floats on the water.

It floats?

The last one didn't float. Are they frozen in more than one type of ice? Is it ice at all? Seems colder than ice.

In any case, this makes it much easier to get it through the door. I push it out, onto the steps, making sure it doesn't slide before pulling myself out.

After the ice is safely inside the Nerve Works, I look back at the sinking house. There's no way I can get another one. The door is almost under the water. I watch as it sinks down to the balcony. Shit, I could have gotten the upstairs girl through the balcony if I saved her for last.

Then the house collapses under the sea.

Never mind. I got as many as I possibly could. Three. I might have saved one or two more, but I fucked up. There wasn't enough time.

At least I got three. I saved three human beings from certain death. I have no idea what they were doing frozen in the garage of that suburban home, but maybe they can tell me. Maybe they have the answers to all my questions.

The water is still bubbling where the house used to be. Still sinking. The chain attached to the house tightens and then the structure's big toe breaks off and splashes into the sea. A cluster of black crabs ooze out of the concrete foot like blood.

The three blocks of ice lie in a row, surrounded by garbage bags full of food. Melting.

They are melting a little quicker now that they are in the warmth. The tattooed girl's arm is completely out of the ice. She is defrosting much quicker than the others. The others are still in block-form.

I sit down next to the tattooed girl and hold her thrashing arm to calm her. But as I take it, I realize she is not tattooed. Her flesh is reptilian.

Throwing the arm away from me and backing up, I watch the arm reaching for me, clawing at the ice to get out of there, to get at me.

They aren't human. They are monsters.

I'm freeing dangerous creatures from their prisons. They are probably some kind of bio-engineered killing machines created for the military, and I'm trapped here with them. If anyone is living in this house, I have killed us all for sure.

Have to move. Have to push these blocks of ice into the sea before they defrost. Before they are able to attack. I push the most-melted one first. The reptilian girl. Pushing the block across the checkered tiles.

"I'm dumping you back into the sea," I tell the monstrous form within the cloudy ice.

But before I get to the steps, the girl's arm wraps around my back, embraces me. I stop. Her touch is relaxing. She holds my frozen hand. Warms it. The blood beneath her skin feels hot.

It comforts me, and I can tell that holding my hand is also a comfort to her. She's just a kid. A scared, helpless kid. I can't kill her, no matter what she is.

I just hold her hand, waiting for her to defrost so I can see what she really is.

I hear footsteps upstairs. Somebody is moving around up there. I let go of the frozen reptile girl. Her fingers wiring at me.

"Hello?" I call out.

The footsteps stop.

"We're down here," I say.

I go to the stairs and climb them.

"I heard your footsteps," I say.

The hallway is still dark. None of the lights in the rooms have turned on. I go back downstairs, looking for other rooms, other ways to get upstairs.

There is one door in a shadowy corner of the vast entrance room. It is white and practically invisible from the other side. I knock first. Not expecting a reply. And open the door. When the door opens a light flickers on like opening a refrigerator. Not quite sure where the light source is coming from. The white walls are reflecting it from somewhere. Also like a refrigerator, the room is cold.

I'm inside one of the thighs of the Nerve Works. It is some kind of wine cellar. There is a window on one side of the room and shelves on the other.

I can't see the ocean through the window. The light reflects my mirror image off of the glass. Can't see anything out there.

The wine racks aren't quite wine racks. They don't seem to actually contain wine. The bottles are the shape of wine bottles, but with clear liquid. I take one from the rack. No label. It isn't corked. It has a cap like a beer bottle.

I slam off the cap against the edge of a shelf and smell the liquid. Smells like alcohol. Like rum and vodka mixed. My hand begins to shake. Liquor. My body has been deprived of liquor, but I've been too excited to notice. I take a drink. Not bad. It's definitely for drinking purposes. I take a chug. Very nice.

Going back to the reptilian girl, I can see her face now. Only a thin layer of glassy ice between us. The other arm is free. Both arms reaching out for me, pulling me close to her. She needs to be comforted. I take a swig of the liquor and sit down on the wet tile floor.

Her face is expressionless under the ice. Eyes wide open. Unable to blink. She is not at all human. Hairless. Earless. Covered in reptile scales. A Frankenstein. The product of a madman. Hopefully the others aren't as horrible as she is.

CHAPTER SEVEN
Snake Woman

"Time to wake up."

A woman's voice. A hand rocking me awake.

I open my eyes to the unfrozen girl standing over me, now completely out of the ice. She stares at me with dark reptilian eyes. A lizard girl. No, not a lizard girl. A snake girl. I can tell by the scales. Her snake tongue flaps out at me, smelling me, as I sit up.

"What's going on?" she asks. "Who are you?"

My head is a bit dizzy. My body must have collapsed from exhaustion. My clothes are now warm and completely dry.

"Conrad," I say. "I have no idea what's going on here. Who are you?"

"Jaji," she says. "I think I have amnesia. I don't know how I got here."

She helps me stand.

"Something is wrong with my skin," she says, feeling her snake scales. "I've changed somehow."

"You weren't born that way?" I ask.

"No," she says, giggling as she feels her skin. "It's all a surprise to me."

I tell her everything that has happened since the human race committed suicide. She laughs at almost everything I say. I'm not sure whether she believes me or not. She doesn't know anything about the laboratory hiding in a suburban garage. She doesn't know how she became a snake girl. She has foggy memories of her past. The last thing she remembers is being a stripper at a club in Detroit with a whole lot of dreams. The last year she remembers is 1974.

"Maybe we should check the place out," she says.

"What about the others?" I say, pointing at the two partially-melted cubes of ice.

"They'll be fine," she says. "We'll only be gone for a few minutes."

"I don't think anyone lives here," Jaji says, as we reach the top of the stairs.

"I heard footsteps," I say. "Somebody has to be here."

"It is too clean and new," she says. "It doesn't look like anyone has ever walked on this carpeting before. There aren't any signs of wear on the tile floor."

"But the lights," I say.

"They could be automatic."

"One of the rooms had a light on inside and the light turned off as I approached it," I say. "Somebody's got to be here."

"Which door?" she asks.

The snake girl flips a switch and the hall lights up. Was that light switch there before? I swear the wall used to be blank. I looked everywhere for a light switch and couldn't find anything.

I point to the seventh door on the right side.

She walks down the hallway. Her snake skin shifting firmly with her steps. I just now realize she is naked. She doesn't seem naked with the scales. But I can see the curves of her ass. Her flesh is lime green with greenish brown stripes. Snakeskin breasts. Snakeskin crotch. Covered yet nude. The flesh on her stomach and between her breasts is the lightest. Almost white. Her belly button is the most human feature on her.

She opens the door I pointed out. Too dark to see. She flips on a light switch.

Empty.

A very clean white room.

"Maybe it was a different room," I say, and open the door next to it. Turn on a light.

Empty.

We go through all of the rooms in the hallway. All of them are just empty and white. No windows. One overhead light. One door. Tan carpeting. That's all.

"Nobody lives here yet," Jaji says.

"Yet?" I ask.

"It seems to have been built recently," she says. "The owners haven't moved in yet."

Owners? Who the hell would move into such a place?

There isn't anything up here besides empty rooms.

I drink my alcohol as the girl checks behind every door. All the same.

"There's got to be a way up to the head," I say. "I saw lights in the windows up there."

"Must be another staircase somewhere," she says.

"Can't be," I say. "There was one door downstairs and this hallway up here. There's no other staircase."

"I want to check downstairs," she says, walking back to the staircase with swaying snake limbs.

The downstairs is not the way we left it. The space has been emptied. The garbage bags of food have disappeared. The two blocks of ice containing the other two frozen girls have disappeared.

"They're gone," she says, standing in the puddle of water where the blocks used to be.

"Where did they go?" I ask.

She shrugs her scaly shoulders.

The front door is closed. I had left it open before. I go outside. No one there. Just black water crashing against the knees of the Nerve Works.

Back inside, we cross the room to the other door.

"This is the only other way they could have gone," I say. "And it is a long room full of liquor bottles." I show her my liquor bottle and take another swig. "No extra staircase. No extra door. Just a dead end."

She opens the door to the liquor room. In the direct center of the room, facing the window, is a staircase. A small black iron staircase spiraling up into the ceiling.

"This wasn't here before!" I cry.

"You must have forgotten," Jaji says.

"But I was just here! I remember going from the window to the bottles . . . I wouldn't have been able to do that if this staircase was here."

She shakes her head at me and goes for the staircase.

At the top of the stairs, we find ourselves in a small circular room surrounded by doors. Jaji goes for the closest door and opens it.

"Anything?" I ask.

She is frozen at the doorway.

Nothing there. Not even a room. It is just a wall. Like the door and doorframe are just decorations for the room. She goes to the next door. Opens it. Nothing. Just wall. Slams it. Goes to the next. Nothing. Slam.

Nothing. Slam. Nothing. Slam.

"What is going on?" she asks.

She opens and slams all the doors. Going in a circle. Checking every door three times around. Until one of the doors opens up into a small room.

"This wasn't here before," she says.

It is a door she has opened twice already. It is no longer a wall. It is a room.

"It's like what happened to me," I say. "Things are appearing on us that weren't there before."

"And disappearing," she says. "The place is haunted."

The room is closet-sized. Empty, except for a ladder. We step inside. The door closes behind us. Looking up: it goes for dozens of feet. Like an elevator shaft. Maybe three or four stories.

"Let's go," I say, setting down my bottle of liquor.

We climb up through the Nerve Works. Probably through the chest and neck of one of the female-shaped structures. Until we arrive in the head.

The heads are conjoined into one room. You can see the reverse side of the woman's face in the walls. It isn't completely empty. There are colorful pillows and rugs in this room. Violet, pink, green, blue. A bright rainbow of colors. Unlike every other room in the mansion.

It is also filled with cats.

"Kitties!" the snake girl says, running at the gang of cats in the room.

Calico cats roam the carpeting, scratch at the rugs, plop down on the pillows. The cats look new to the room. There is no cat hair anywhere. The pillows and rugs are brand new. Yet the cats are just now tearing into them. Their hair sheds all over the floor. It's as if nothing in here existed until we entered the room.

Jaji runs after the cats. She catches one and hugs it to her scaly breasts, but it hisses and wiggles out of her grip. Jaji laughs and goes for another one.

I examine the room. There are two large windows on each side, in the area of the back of the skull where the twins are conjoined.

On the other side of one of the large windows is a balcony.

There isn't a door to the balcony. The window doesn't open. But there is a balcony out there full of plants, flowers, and dozens of varieties of butterfly. A few calico cats are out there, even though there isn't a passageway for them to get in and out. The cats swat at the butterflies and scratch at the glass.

"Nobody's up here," she says, giving up on trying to pet the cats.

"The other two girls had to have gone somewhere," I say. "They must have come up here."

"There's another way," she says, pointing at a small door on the other side of the room.

I cross the room to check it out.

The other door just leads to a bathroom. A small, cramped bathroom. And instead of clean and empty like all the other rooms in the house, this one is cluttered with junk. Old brown and red towels hang on a towel rack. Other towels are wet and wadded up on the floor. A medicine cabinet packed with junk. Used Q-tips in the sink. Old toothbrushes inside of a jar. Bars of soap. Tampons. Used tissues. A picnic blanket draped over the shower curtain.

"What do you think those cats eat?" Jaji asks. "There weren't any bowls of food or any water. No litter boxes either."

I don't answer. Something is off. Looking at myself in the mirror, I don't see my reflection. Somebody else is in there instead of me.

"What's wrong?" Jaji asks, looking over my shoulder.

The mirror must be broken.

"I'm not me," I say.

"You look like you to me," she says.

Then I realize. It *is* me. An earlier version of me. I'm young. I'm in my thirties again. No, maybe even my twenties.

"I'm young again," I say.

"That's how you've always looked," she says.

"I used to be old."

"I don't know anything about that," she says. "You haven't changed while I've known you. But I guess that's not been very long."

I feel my smooth face, touch my dark brown hair. It's real. I'm young again.

"A door?" Jaji asks.

I look at her and she points to a small wooden door inside of the shower. Just under the shower head. Jaji opens the door and crawls through.

I continue looking at myself in the mirror. Young again! This place isn't haunted. It's magic. I can't stop smiling at myself.

We reach a dead end with this room. It is a nice large bedroom with fuzzy tan carpeting and blankets on the floor. Eyehole windows. Jaji lies onto the blankets, stretching her body out. Then she screams.

The blankets levitate her off of the floor and a bed grows from the carpet, right underneath her. She leaps out of the bed as it forms itself. The sheets and blankets fold around the mattress. Long metal bars lock together to form the frame. Pillows puff out from below the sheets like popcorn.

It stops. The bed is finished. We watch it, waiting for something else to happen.

"This place . . ." I say. "It seems like it's being built around us. Like someone is creating it piece by piece as we explore."

"It's magical," Jaji says, widening her reptilian eyes.

Jaji collapses on the bed.

"Don't lie on it," I cry.

"Why not?" she asks. "It was created for us."

"We don't know what it was created for," I say.

"I'm tired," she says. "I want to sleep. In the morning I bet the house will be finished."

"How can you sleep?" I ask. "You've been asleep for thirty years."

"Yeah, and I feel like I can sleep thirty more."

I take off my yellow sweater and lie down next to her, plopping my head right into the pillow. I'm tired as well. Very tired. I don't even remember the last time I had a decent night's sleep.

Jaji wraps her body around me. Her snake flesh is firm but smooth, limbs hugging me close to her, gripping me like a boa constrictor.

"I bet it will be all finished in the morning," she says. "A magical castle for us to live in."

She squeezes tighter.

I can hear her smiling as the air is compressed out of my lungs.

CHAPTER EIGHT
New Home

I wake to the feeling of warmth and wetness. Like I am having sex. My penis inside of a juicy vagina.

I open my eyes and look down. The snake girl has me in her mouth. Her lips are stretched out three times the size of her head and wrapped around me. She's swallowing me, up to my thighs. Her arms wrapped around my waist, pulling me down into her.

Her eyes roll back behind her eyelids, like she is getting sexual pleasure out of this. My toes wiggling inside of her squishy belly cause her to moan.

"What are you doing," I scream.

She freezes. Her eyes open and look at me, bashfully. Then she slips my legs out of her throat and wipes the saliva from her lips.

"Were you trying to eat me?" I cry.

"No," she says. "I just wanted to see how far I could get you."

She smiles at me.

"Isn't it neat?" she asks, as she grabs her lips and stretches out her mouth at me. "I really *am* like a snake!"

"Don't do that again," I say.

I step out of the bed.

"Aw, don't get mad," she says. "I wouldn't really eat you, even if I could fit you all the way inside."

The room has changed overnight. It's no longer just a

bed. It now has dressers, mirrors, nightstands, paintings of seascapes, and a closet full of clothes.

I go right for the closet. It is mostly fancy suits and dresses.

"Oooohhh," Jaji says at the new clothes. She takes out a red dress and presses it against her body, asking me if it will look good on her.

I blink at her. She laughs and squeezes her shoulders in response to my blink, as if my blink meant "You will look wonderful in that!"

She has me try on a black suit. It fits perfectly. White shirt. Black bow tie. Almost as nice as a tuxedo.

We get dressed. The snake woman looks completely awkward in her dress, but she wears it anyway. Her feet won't fit comfortably in any of the shoes so she has to walk barefoot. We go through the door to the bathroom. The knees of our outfits get wet. We use the bathroom in front of each other like we've been a couple for years, and clean ourselves up with deodorant and perfumes from the medicine cabinet.

"Where to?" I ask.

"That way," she says, pointing to the door. "Time to explore our new home."

The cat room is now centered with a long dining table, covered in margarine flowers and sweet breakfast meats. The morning sun shines through the windows and brightens the room. The cats are lying on pillowy chairs, bathing in the warm orange sun. Some of them are walking on the table, licking the meats and drinking water from wine glasses.

Jaji takes a rolled slice of meat and slurps it down.

"Tangy," she says.

There are two girls on the other end of the table, peaking at us from behind the floral arrangements.

"Hey," Jaji calls out. "Who are you?"

Upon closer inspection, we notice they are like Jaji. They aren't quite human.

One is a dog girl: half Dalmatian, half woman. Her head is that of a dog's and her body from the neck down is that of a woman's but covered in white fur with black spots. She pants her tongue at us while cutting meats on her plate with a knife and fork.

The other woman is hiding behind her chair, slinking away from us. She looks more human than the other. She is a bird girl. A falcon. Her face is human, but she has falcon feathers instead of hair. The feathers grow down her sides and back but don't cover her breasts, so she blocks my view of them with her arms.

"Did you come out of the ice?" I ask.

The falcon girl shrugs.

Jaji pushes me back and approaches the girl. She must be eighteen or nineteen years old, maybe younger.

"What's your name?" the snake woman asks her.

The girl squats down behind her chair.

"Hey," Jaji says, taking her by the hand and lifting her up. "It's okay. You're safe now." She sits her in the chair and pets her feathery head. "You're with friends."

The girl drinks liquor from a wine glass.

"I'm Kara," she says, then scratches the dog girl behind the ear. "She used to be my friend Jen, but she doesn't remember me." The dog licks her hand. "Now I call her Doggy . . . or Spots. It's easier that way."

Unlike Jaji, Kara remembers what happened to her.

"It was a big operation," she says. "They would abduct junkies and prostitutes off the street and put us into cages. We thought it was some kind of white slavery ring at first, but then they started hooking us up to machines and injecting us with stuff. That's when we started changing. Jen said they were messing with our DNA, turning us into hybrids."

"Why did they do that to you?" I ask.

"Sex," Jaji says.

Kara nods at the snake woman. "They were turning us into genetically enhanced whores to be sold to perverted rich men."

"With exotic tastes in women," Jaji adds.

The dog girl licks her black nose at me.

"Last thing I remember is some woman telling me they were going to freeze me in ice and put me in storage until they found a buyer interested in my breed. I have no idea how long ago that was."

"The year is 2004," I say.

"It's been thirteen years," she says.

Jaji and I spend the afternoon exploring the house. It is larger than before. New staircases have sprouted up, leading to new wings. There are new living rooms, new luxurious bedrooms, kitchens, dining rooms. Everything completely furnished and comfortable.

The empty rooms downstairs now look lived in, like their occupants are just out to work and are expected back soon.

"The question is," I say, "are all these things being created for us, or somebody else who hasn't arrived yet?"

Jaji shrugs. "Maybe both."

Calico cats are everywhere, infesting the house like cockroaches.

"But they're cute furry cockroaches," Jaji says.

I was never a fan of cats. More of a dog person. Good old bull dogs, that's what I love. Tough little buggers, they are. Not afraid to fart.

At lunch time, all the dining rooms in the house fill with Italian sandwiches and onion soups. We load them up on a tray and take it outside for a picnic by the sea. There's not much room outside. Just the front steps leading into the water. Miles and miles of water. Waves crash against the building's knees.

Breathing in the salty sea air as I eat my sandwich, I say, "What are we supposed to do?"

"Enjoy ourselves," she says. "We've been given a second chance at life. Let's make the most of it."

"None of this is right," I say.

"You think I don't know that?" she says. "I'm the one who has been frozen for thirty years. I'm the one who has scales instead of skin."

She rubs her skin at me.

We watch the water for a while. Seagulls made of ground beef perch on the thigh of the Nerve Works. The orange sun oozes gently out of the sky.

CHAPTER NINE
Lonely Vacation

Days pass.

We stop questioning the mysteries of our predicament and try to have fun. It's like we're on vacation. We eat and relax during the day, swim in the ocean, then drink all night. I've been sleeping in the arms of the snake woman every night, but we do not make love. I am still uncomfortable with the fact that she's part reptile and she is still uncomfortable with the fact that I used to be elderly.

"It takes time," she says. "We'll grow on one another."

But we are still able to hold each other in the night. Her warmth is comforting and keeps me sane. I'm beginning to get used to the feel of her scales against my skin.

Jaji finds a stereo and wants to dance with me. I'm drunk enough to agree. She puts on a white ballroom gown and has me wear a tux. The music playing on the radio is older than me. From the twenties probably. The radio station plays only one song over and over again. There isn't an announcer on the air. We don't know where the waves are coming from.

It's a slow song, so we slow dance. She coils her limbs around me and snuggles her bald snake head into my chest. I don't attempt any fancy moves, just rock side to side. It is nice though. I stare down at her scaly skull like it is some kind of pulsating alien egg.

"What were you like before?" she asks me.

"Old," I say. "Just an old man."

"But what did you do?" she asks. "Everyone has their passions. Everyone has something that drives them through life. Kids? Art? Work?"

"I didn't have any of those," I say.

"What did you do for a living?" she asks.

"I worked in packaging for thirty years. Then retired."

"Were you in a war?"

"Nope."

"Have any hobbies?"

"When I was a kid, maybe. I drank a lot and watched TV."

"You were so boring."

"I was old. There wasn't anything to do. I was just waiting to die."

"Then why didn't you?" she says.

I smile at her. I was hoping she would say that.

She spins herself around and then returns to my arms, facing me now. Looking into me with her cold black reptilian eyes, smelling me with her long flapping tongue.

"What about you?" I ask. "What did you do?"

"What didn't I do?" she says.

"Weren't you just a stripper?" I ask.

"Nobody is *just* a stripper," she says. "Maybe you can be *just* an old man, but I've never met a stripper who didn't lead a complex and interesting life."

"So what was your complex and interesting life all about?" I ask.

"Collecting," she says.

"What's so interesting about that?" I ask.

"I collect memories," she says. "I'm like an artist. Only instead of paintings, instead of sculptures, my experiences are my masterpieces. I live my life in constant spontaneity. One day I'll be pretending to be a theater student in California, the next I'll be hitchhiking to Texas with a gay football coach who knits little hats for invisible babies."

"Everyone has stories like that."

"Obviously, you don't," she says. "Otherwise you wouldn't be *just* an old man. I've lived for a third as long as you and I already have more interesting stories than a novel could possibly contain."

"Wait until you get old and start losing all of those stories, or just stop giving a fuck about them. Then you'll understand why I'm *just* an old man."

Jaji smirks at me. She has a cute way of wrinkling the bridge of her nose when she's annoyed. If only she wasn't such a snake.

Kara is very shy. She took up residence in the farthest room away from us and hardly ever eats or talks to us. Sometimes Jaji can get her to speak, but she's not interested in socializing. She drinks herself to sleep every night, all alone in her tiny room. Living like I used to live.

"What do you think is wrong with her?" I ask Jaji, salting my toes.

Jaji is busy painting a masterpiece on the wall with colored goop she found inside clam shells hidden behind a board under a bathroom sink.

"I mean, she's kind of weird," I say.

"She's had a hard life," Jaji says.

I scrunch the salt between my toes. It makes a loud enough noise to get Jaji's attention. She frowns at my wiggling piggies.

"Everyone's had a hard life," I say.

"She was abused as a child," she says. "You can tell by the way she curls her skin and tries to rub the air off of her arms and out of her hair. Probably molested and beaten by her mom or stepdad. I don't think she's ever been loved."

Jaji steps back to show me her painting. It is a painting of me and her, Kara and the dog girl, holding hands around a Christmas tree.

For some reason I say, "Maybe we should try to make her feel loved."

The dog girl sleeps on Kara's floor at night, but she seems to prefer our company during the day. Her brain is like a dog's brain, so she mostly just likes to play fetch and chase the cats around the living room.

Sometimes she forgets her size and tries to jump in my lap, licking my face. I push her off so she doesn't crush me with her weight, but then she gets sad and won't forgive me until I pet her or scratch under her chin.

"She can be your pet and Zombi will be mine," Jaji says, holding up a little calico kitty with a black face.

Dalmatian Girl pants at me. She is kind of a cute doggy, despite the fact that she has breasts. But I'd rather have a bull dog.

"So what did you make her?" Jaji asks.

We are making presents for Kara to cheer her up. It's my fault for giving the snake girl the stupid idea. If Kara is anything like me she just wants to be left alone. Nothing pisses me off more than somebody trying to cheer me up.

"I made her a head," I say.

I hold up a head.

We found stacks of newspapers inside of a mattress and decided to make papier-mâché presents for Kara. The doggy girl rests her cheek on my knee as I dip newspaper strips in a pool of glue that has been dripping out of the chandelier.

"A head?" Jaji asks.

I didn't know what else to make. It's just a head. No hair, no neck. Buttons for eyes. Huge heart-shaped lips.

"It looks retarded," she says.

"Yeah . . ." I say, taking a sip of liquor.

She is making a Christmas tree. Paying close attention to the details. Making little ornaments to hang on the branches. Painting them with her leftover clamshell goop. "This has to cheer her up," Jaji says. "Christmas trees make everyone happy."

Jaji, dressed in fuzzy teddy bear pajamas, knocks on Kara's door holding her little Christmas tree like a birthday cake.

There's no answer.

"Kara, are you here?"

No answer.

"Come on, Kara, we have surprises for you."

We wait for a response . . .

"Go away," says a crackling voice from the other side of the door.

"What, you don't *want* your presents?" Jaji asks, bending her hip, irritated.

No answer.

"She's probably sleeping," I say. "Let her be."

"No!" Jaji hisses at me.

She pounds hard on the door with her elbow until it opens.

"What?" Kara asks.

Her feathers smashed to one side. Eyes rolling back. She must have drank herself to sleep and we just woke her up.

"Presents?" Jaji says with a fanged smile.

Kara squints at her. "You woke me up for this?"

Jaji hands her the present, still smiling, but Kara holds it upside-down. Like she doesn't know what it is. Many of the ornaments fall off and break on the stone tile floor.

"Think I care about this?" Kara asks.

She tosses the Christmas tree over our heads.

"What the hell's your problem?" Jaji screams.

"Right now, you are," Kara says.

I hide my present behind my back.

"Why can't you just let yourself be happy?" Jaji cries. "Why do you have to mope around all day?"

"What's there to be happy about?" she asks.

"Look," Jaji says, flipping her tongue in frustration. "I'm trying to make the most of a bad situation."

"Leave me out of it," she says, and closes the door in Jaji's face.

Jaji's green face is turning red.

"Don't bother me again," Kara says through the door.

"Fine, be miserable!" Jaji says.

No response.

"She's just drunk," I say.

"Forget her," Jaji says. "She can be alone and miserable for all I care."

Jaji reclaims her papier-mâché Christmas tree and hugs it to her chest.

"Let's go skinny dipping in the moonlight," she says.

Jaji takes me outside. The ocean air drenches me with icy moisture that makes my nose run. She slips off her fuzzy pajamas and dives into the dark water. Jaji swims through the waves like a sea serpent.

"Come on," she says, teeth chattering. "It's amazing."

"It's got to be freezing," I say.

"It is!" she says, holding her chest. "Come in with me."

"No way," I say. "Come back inside."

"You're such a boring old man!" she says, and swims away.

Like any vacation, it eventually becomes tiresome and monotonous, and I long to go home. I cope by drowning my boredom with alcohol.

Jaji takes the bottle out of my hand. "You're done with that."

"Huh?" I say, trying to push away her cat as it claws onto the back of my chair.

"You can drink three days a week, like me. The rest of the week you'll have to find something else to do."

"Why?"

"You're becoming pathetic."

When did I stop being pathetic?

I tell her, "I don't know what else to do."

"Try reading," she says, nuzzling her face into Zombi's belly and then placing her off to the side.

She stands me up out of the lazy boy chair I've been sitting in and pulls off the seat cushion. Underneath where I had been sitting, there is a hatch. I've never seen this before. Jaji opens it like a manhole to reveal a ladder going down into a brightly lit chamber.

"What is down there?" I ask.

"The library," she says.

There are hundreds of books down here. Red and green vines crawl across the bookshelves and up the walls.

Jaji plops me down at a wooden desk where caterpillars and tiny blue snails play.

"Here." She hands me a book.

I read the cover. "The Little Prince?"

"Yeah," she says. "I love that book."

"It's a kid's book," I say.

"It's a special book," she says. "Maybe the best book I've ever read."

Then she goes off to find a book for herself.

I've never been a big reader of fiction. Why the hell would anyone want to read about things that never even happened?

I humor her and pretend to read the book. I'm too drunk to actually read. The words make me dizzy.

"Who did this to you?" I hear Jaji say from across the library.

I put the book down and cross the room to find Kara curled up between the bookshelves, Jaji trying to comfort her.

The girl's pink clothes are ripped, her face covered with cuts and bruises.

"Did you do this?" the snake girl cries at me.

"No," I say.

"How could you?" she yells at me.

"It wasn't him," the falcon girl says.

"Who then?" Jaji asks.

"The white queen," she says. "She comes to my bedroom at night. At first, I thought she was a dream. I welcomed her. But then she started to get mean. She started hurting me."

The snake girl coils around her. "Where is she now?"

The falcon girl shakes her head and cries into Jaji's scaly breasts.

CHAPTER TEN
Cobweb Dreams

We try not to let Kara out of our sight for the next few days, but she is such a private person. She refuses to spend more than five minutes with us at a time. Her bruises seem to get worse and worse every morning, her cheeks and eyes swollen, but she won't talk about it.

One day her face is so swollen that she can hardly see through her eyes, can hardly open her mouth. She won't let us see her anymore.

"Something serious is going on," Jaji says.

"Do you think there's somebody else here?" I ask.

"No," she says. "It's this place. I think it's rejecting her."

"How?"

"She doesn't fit in. She's not happy like we are. I think the house doesn't want her here."

"You think this place is alive?"

"It *feels* alive," she says. "You know it feels alive. It mutates and changes and seems to have an awareness. I think this white queen she is seeing is like a white blood cell. It is the house's immune system and thinks Kara is a virus."

"What are we going to do?" I ask.

"Get her out of here," she says.

"How? Where is she supposed to go?"

"We'll think of something."

One night, passed out at the end of one of my drinking nights, I have a bad dream:

I dream that I'm being smothered to death in a wet plastic bag. It's wrapped around me so tightly that I can't move my arms, my knees pressed against my chest. I try struggling but my muscles aren't working right, the lack of oxygen causes me to lose consciousness. Then I dream about fishing with my old bull dog. Zombi is there too, for some reason.

When I wake up I'm covered with sweat and see that Jaji is trying to swallow me again. Her mouth is covering my ankles. She slides my feet out of her and lies down next to me, facing the other way, pretending she's asleep.

I sit up. "What were you doing?"

She pretends she's half asleep. "Huh?"

"You—" I begin.

"No, I wasn't," she says.

"Damn you," I say to her and bounce out of the bed.

She sits up and tries to hold my hand.

"I'm sorry," she cries. "It's my snake DNA kicking in. It only happens when I'm really horny."

"Why don't you masturbate then?" I say, drying off the moisture from my arms with a sheet.

"Masturbating isn't enough anymore," she says. "I need some real sex."

"Why don't you try seducing me when you're horny instead of trying to swallow me?" I say.

Pause.

She bursts into giggles and bounces on the bed. "I was

able to get you all the way in this time!"

"I can't believe you," I say, searching the floor for my pants.

"It was amazing!" Tears are flowing out of her eyes and she can't stop smiling. "You were actually inside of me! My belly was as big as the whole bed!"

I put on a robe. It's her fluffy flowery robe, but I don't care. "You could have killed me."

"No, I wouldn't," she says, she reaches out to hold my hand. Like it's some kind of special moment that she wants to share with me.

"Don't touch me," I say, and leave the room.

I go out onto the steps in the front of the house and drink some more liquor out under the stars. Good thing I've got a never-ending supply of this stuff in the pantry.

Sitting against one of the stone butt cheeks, I watch the moon reflect against the calm water. All the lights are off in the house. Usually, the house keeps them on for us. But now it's dark inside. Maybe the house knows I want to enjoy the moonlight.

I hear a faint moaning coming from somewhere inside, like somebody's having sex. Probably Jaji masturbating, getting it out of her system. It fades away after awhile. Could have been my imagination.

The alcohol feels nice, buzzing through me with the relaxing sound of the water. My eyes drift shut. A splashing sound wakes me before I lose consciousness. The moon has disappeared from the sky. I can't see anything. Disoriented.

No, the moon hasn't disappeared, something is blocking it. I see thousands of black hands reaching out, waving at me like jellyfish.

My nostrils thicken with the scent of pennies and rotten fish as the mass of limbs and tentacles puffs air at me. It belches out a roar that vibrates through the concrete steps and my spine. Then it sinks down into the soup.

The moon reappears in the sky and my vision clears.

That thing must have been huge. As big as the entire building.

I stagger back inside and look for a place to sleep. There are bedrooms under every brick in this place.

A loud moan.

It is in the room with me. I look around. The lights are off, but the moonlight shining through the windows is light enough. More moaning. It isn't Jaji.

Upstairs.

I see her on the staircase.

The falcon girl is pressed against the steps, bare-chested, moaning in pleasure. I don't see anyone with her until I get closer, get the right view in the moonlight. The figure on top of her looks like it's made of gas, almost transparent. The longer I watch it, the more its shape fills in.

The white queen.

The apparition is at least ten feet tall entombing Kara with its body. White tentacles twist out of the ghost's belly, they swim through the air around the girl. Some tentacles are wrapped around her arms and thighs. One tentacle caresses her feathery vagina.

Kara's face is extremely swollen. Twice the size it used to be. Her facial features have become so fat that they are overlapped each other. It makes her head look like a baseball glove.

A white tentacle smears grease on her fat facial features, searching the folds for a hole. The falcon girl coos as the tentacle finds its way into her mouth. She sucks on it, tries to breathe as it slides down her throat.

As grotesque as it looks, they both seem to be enjoying it. The way Kara moans, the way her larynx vibrates against the tentacle in her throat, the way she wiggles and stretches. I can't get myself to break them up. Just watching. Not able to look away as my legs take me out of the room.

I tell Jaji about it and she nods her head.

"I knew it," she says.

"Knew what?"

She nods her head at me.

We find the falcon girl trying to drink the pain away. She can hardly fit the bottle through the bloating of her face to reach her mouth. She can hardly see through her pinhole eyes.

"See, like a basketball," I say to the snake woman.

She waves away my words.

"What is she doing to you?" Jaji asks the girl, sitting down on a flower table next to her.

Kara slurps and wheezes.

"Why didn't you tell us?"

The falcon girl tries to cover her enormous face.

"We need to get her out of here," Jaji tells me. "Before it kills her. Or find a way to stop it."

The snake girl pets Kara's feathers and walks away. I follow.

Before we leave the room, the girl says, "She says she loves me."

Jaji stops, turns around to see the bruised and beaten girl hugging her knees to her chin.

"And I think I love her too," she says.

CHAPTER ELEVEN
The Queen of Cats

For several days, Jaji and I search the house for signs of the white queen.

"She's like a ghost," I say. "She could be in a different dimension. The ghost dimension."

"Don't be a jackass," she says.

We keep looking.

Kara's head has swelled even larger. It is now as big as her torso. Instead of scrunching her facial features together, now the swelling has stretched them out. Like her face has been blown up like a balloon.

She's bedridden.

Jaji makes a bed for her by the dining table outside of our bedroom. She wants to keep an eye on her, just in case the white queen comes back. Kara is too weak to speak and rarely stays conscious for more than an hour a day.

We spend most of the time waiting around to see what happens. Doggy Girl wags her tail at me, wondering what all the fuss is about.

"We should have gotten her out of here when we had the chance," Jaji says.

"How?" I say.

"I don't know, we could have built a raft."

Jaji pets Dog Girl's furry breasts to see what they feel like, and I sneer at her for doing it. Dog Girl doesn't seem to notice.

"She would have died out there," I tell her.

Jaji orders me to stay awake in the dining room and keep an eye on Kara. She goes back to bed and snuggles Dog Girl to sleep.

I told her no but I'm out here in the dining room anyway. Too dehydrated to drink alcohol, but that doesn't stop me. Worst part of dehydration is the headache and alcohol's good at curing headaches.

Calico cats swarm the table as I drink, meowing at me like I have food to give them. Jaji's little kitten, Zombi, climbs my shirt and sits on my shoulder. Doesn't look at me, just perches on my shoulder like a parrot.

I rest my head against it drunkenly and the cat meows at me. Mad at me for throwing it off balance. It lies down on my shoulder and my head rolls onto its back. The kitten makes a good pillow. I close my eyes and the cat's purrs calm my aching headache.

When my eyes open I see the white ghostly form hovering over Kara. I hop to my feet, not sure what I'm supposed to do to stop her. I circle the table and wave my arms at her and make buzzing sounds, trying to scare her off. Zombi is still on my shoulder, claws digging into my clothes for balance.

The white queen turns to me. A young woman's face.

"Shhhh!" says the apparition, a metallic whisper. "She's in labor."

I quiet down and watch. Not sure what else to do.

Kara is whining, half-conscious. There is bubbling inside of her enormous head. Her cartoonishly stretched mouth screams as the bubbling gets stronger. I step back. Sweat pours down her skin and her limbs quiver.

The white queen smiles from above as the falcon girl's skull cracks open like an egg. The fracture starts at her forehead and splits her face in half. Kara continues to scream, still alive, as baby cats crawl out of her face. Dozens of them. Slimy kittens smaller than my fist pull themselves out of her head and across her sweaty sheets.

"My babies," the apparition hisses.

Kara's eyeballs drop out of her flaps of face. Her mouth stops making noise, but her lips continue fluttering. She dies slowly in the puddle of baby cats. Her head becomes completely hollow. Just a big empty leather bag. The white queen smiles at her little ones and kisses Kara's dead body with each of her white tentacles.

I slip into the bathroom and lock myself in. The cat still on my shoulder. It jumps off onto the toilet seat and meows at me as I crawl through the door in the shower to Jaji. But the room is empty. Neither the snake girl nor Dog Girl are here.

"Jaji?" I call out.

No reply.

They couldn't have left the room. There's no other way out.

I look for secret doors in the corners and the closet. Behind the dresser. Under the bed. Wait a minute . . .

I look under the bed again.

Jaji's face is staring back at me.

"Go away," she says.

Her chest and belly are stretched out. She hugs the bottom of her bulge. Her eyes close.

"What did you do?" I ask.

"Shhh," she says. "I'm digesting."

"Kara's dead," I tell her.

She hushes me again. "Leave me alone for a few days."

I step away from her and grind my teeth.

Pacing the room, agitated, I wish there was a place that was safe for me.

"I'm sorry I ate your dog," she says. "I just had to see what it felt like."

I open the door to leave.

"You should be happy," she says to me as I crawl into the bathtub. "I probably would have eaten you if your dog wasn't here."

Sitting in the bathtub, not wanting to go into the bedroom with the snake woman or into the dining room with the ghost. A couple hours pass. I can't sleep. Zombie keeps meowing at me to open the door.

Perhaps the apparition has left the room . . .

I enter the dining room. Moonlight reflects against the silverware and vases. Kara's body is being absorbed into the floor. Pink oatmeal rises out of the carpeting like stomach acids, breaking down her flesh to fluids. The pile of kittens she birthed are licking up her melted parts as the house takes her in.

The white queen lowers from the ceiling above me and I leap out of the way, tripping over Zombi and falling to the floor. Before I can crawl away, she wraps her white tentacles around me. They flow electricity into my skin, a tranquilizing effect.

Her voice is more human now. Motherly.

"Don't worry," she says. "I'm not going to impregnate you."

I try to pull free but my muscles are limp.

"You're the last male," she says. "I need you to repopulate the human species."

She takes her tentacles off of me and examines my body. Zombi lies on my back and purrs herself to sleep.

"Who are you?" I ask, my voice soggy.

She brings her face close to mine. Her skin is smooth and white, but hollow inside. She doesn't seem ghostly, her skin is just so thin it is almost transparent. Like the tissue of a jellyfish.

"I am the Queen of Cats," she says, petting Zombi with a tentacle.

Zombi meows with her eyes closed.

"I used to impregnate sailors with my seed," she says. "But there aren't any sailors left. As far as I know, all humans besides you and your friends have died out."

She points at the door. She probably doesn't know that one of my friends has eaten the other.

"You must repopulate your species," she says. "Without mankind I cannot reproduce myself. I cannot make more of my babies."

Zombi meows like she can tell the Queen of Cats is smiling at her.

"I will provide you with eternal youth," she says. "You will never get sick, never grow old. You and your woman will live forever, as long as you keep producing children for me to mate with."

"What if I refuse?" I tell her.

Her tentacles drape around me again, pumping more electricity into me. My body becomes so limp it feels like it will fall through the floor.

She says, "If you ever disobey me I will incapacitate both you and your woman. I will take your arms, your legs, your eyes, your tongue, all of your senses. You will become breeding machines for me. You will live that way for an eternity."

Drool pours out of the side of my lips.

"Or you can live in eternal paradise," she says. "Anything you want, it's yours. Luxury, entertainment, adventure. Anything you can imagine, I can create."

I can't speak anymore.

Consciousness drifts away from me . . .

CHAPTER TWELVE
Bitter Paradise

After Jaji is done digesting the dog girl a few days later, we start making babies.

She gave us our lives. Saved us from death and will continue to save us from death for a very long time. We owe it to her to do what she wants. But what kind of life has she given us? To watch our children die violently century after century? Raped night after night by the Queen of Cats?

It will surely tear Jaji apart. She will have to stay pregnant almost constantly. It will probably be worse than hell for her. But right now she is happy. She is excited to see our baby. Excited to see if it will be half-snake.

She thinks the Queen of Cats will allow her to keep some of the children. She thinks there has to be a way to look positively at all this.

Jaji smiles at me every time she tells me to stay positive. I'm beginning to realize how beautiful she is, even though she's a snake, even though she ate the dog woman.

Jaji's belly is stretched out like she's swallowed a few cats. We picnic on a thigh of the Nerve Works, lounging in the bright blue. Water crashes against the building, spraying us with a refreshing mist that I swear smells like olives.

Zombi is fully grown, balancing on the kneecap, squinting her eyes at the wind and hoping a fish will jump out of the water nearby.

I'm trying to read The Little Prince again, lying on my back with a martini in my hand. It's actually pretty fun to drink while you read, if you're only a little buzzed.

It's going to be Halloween in a few days. Jaji is carving a pumpkin, sticky with orange goop and seeds all over her snake scales.

"What are you going to dress up as?" she asks me.

Zombi crawls onto my chest so that I can't see the book I'm trying to read. Then meows in my face.

"We're dressing up?" I ask.

"Yeah," she says. "You have to dress up on Halloween."

I chug my drink. It refills itself as I set it down on the knee.

"Kika can make you any costume you want," she says. Kika is her nickname for the Queen of Cats. "I'm going as a fairy princess."

She smiles snake fangs at me. She's already a Halloween costume.

"I haven't thought about it yet," I say. "Maybe a werewolf."

"Yeah," she says, smiling at the cat-shaped pumpkin in her lap. "Werewolves are always best."

ABOUT THE AUTHOR

Carlton Mellick III is one of the leading authors in the new *Bizarro* genre uprising. Since 2001, his surreal counterculture novels have drawn an international cult following despite the fact that they have been shunned by most libraries and corporate bookstores. He lives in Portland, OR, the bizarro fiction mecca.

Visit him online at **www.carltonmellick.com**

BIZARRO BOOKS

CATALOG   FALL 2011

**ERASERHEAD
PRESS**

Your major resource for the bizarro fiction genre:

WWW.BIZARROCENTRAL.COM

Introduce yourselves to the bizarro fiction genre and all of its authors with the Bizarro Starter Kit series. Each volume features short novels and short stories by ten of the leading bizarro authors, designed to give you a perfect sampling of the genre for only $10.

BB-0X1
"The Bizarro Starter Kit" (Orange)
Featuring D. Harlan Wilson, Carlton Mellick III, Jeremy Robert Johnson, Kevin L Donihe, Gina Ranalli, Andre Duza, Vincent W. Sakowski, Steve Beard, John Edward Lawson, and Bruce Taylor. **236 pages $10**

BB-0X2
"The Bizarro Starter Kit" (Blue)
Featuring Ray Fracalossy, Jeremy C. Shipp, Jordan Krall, Mykle Hansen, Andersen Prunty, Eckhard Gerdes, Bradley Sands, Steve Aylett, Christian TeBordo, and Tony Rauch. **244 pages $10**

BB-0X2
"The Bizarro Starter Kit" (Purple)
Featuring Russell Edson, Athena Villaverde, David Agranoff, Matthew Revert, Andrew Goldfarb, Jeff Burk, Garrett Cook, Kris Saknussemm, Cody Goodfellow, and Cameron Pierce **264 pages $10**

BB-001 **"The Kafka Effekt"** **D. Harlan Wilson** - A collection of forty-four irreal short stories loosely written in the vein of Franz Kafka, with more than a pinch of William S. Burroughs sprinkled on top. **211 pages** **$14**

BB-002 **"Satan Burger"** **Carlton Mellick III** - The cult novel that put Carlton Mellick III on the map ... Six punks get jobs at a fast food restaurant owned by the devil in a city violently overpopulated by surreal alien cultures. **236 pages** **$14**

BB-003 **"Some Things Are Better Left Unplugged"** **Vincent Sakwoski** - Join The Man and his Nemesis, the obese tabby, for a nightmare roller coaster ride into this postmodern fantasy. **152 pages** **$10**

BB-004 **"Shall We Gather At the Garden?"** **Kevin L Donihe** - Donihe's Debut novel. Midgets take over the world, The Church of Lionel Richie vs. The Church of the Byrds, plant porn and more! **244 pages** **$14**

BB-005 **"Razor Wire Pubic Hair"** **Carlton Mellick III** - A genderless humandildo is purchased by a razor dominatrix and brought into her nightmarish world of bizarre sex and mutilation. **176 pages** **$11**

BB-006 **"Stranger on the Loose"** **D. Harlan Wilson** - The fiction of Wilson's 2nd collection is planted in the soil of normalcy, but what grows out of that soil is a dark, witty, otherworldly jungle... **228 pages** **$14**

BB-007 **"The Baby Jesus Butt Plug"** **Carlton Mellick III** - Using clones of the Baby Jesus for anal sex will be the hip sex fetish of the future. **92 pages** **$10**

BB-008 **"Fishyfleshed"** **Carlton Mellick III** - The world of the past is an illogical flatland lacking in dimension and color, a sick-scape of crispy squid people wandering the desert for no apparent reason. **260 pages** **$14**

BB-009 **"Dead Bitch Army" Andre Duza** - Step into a world filled with racist teenagers, cannibals, 100 warped Uncle Sams, automobiles with razor-sharp teeth, living graffiti, and a pissed-off zombie bitch out for revenge. **344 pages $16**

BB-010 **"The Menstruating Mall" Carlton Mellick III** - "The Breakfast Club meets Chopping Mall as directed by David Lynch." - Brian Keene **212 pages $12**

BB-011 **"Angel Dust Apocalypse" Jeremy Robert Johnson** - Meth-heads, man-made monsters, and murderous Neo-Nazis. "Seriously amazing short stories..." - Chuck Palahniuk, author of Fight Club **184 pages $11**

BB-012 **"Ocean of Lard" Kevin L Donihe / Carlton Mellick III** - A parody of those old Choose Your Own Adventure kid's books about some very odd pirates sailing on a sea made of animal fat. **176 pages $12**

BB-015 **"Foop!" Chris Genoa** - Strange happenings are going on at Dactyl, Inc, the world's first and only time travel tourism company. "A surreal pie in the face!" - Christopher Moore **300 pages $14**

BB-020 **"Punk Land" Carlton Mellick III** - In the punk version of Heaven, the anarchist utopia is threatened by corporate fascism and only Goblin, Mortician's sperm, and a blue-mohawked female assassin named Shark Girl can stop them. **284 pages $15**

BB-021 **"Pseudo-City" D. Harlan Wilson** - Pseudo-City exposes what waits in the bathroom stall, under the manhole cover and in the corporate boardroom, all in a way that can only be described as mind-bogglingly irreal. **220 pages $16**

BB-023 **"Sex and Death In Television Town" Carlton Mellick III** - In the old west, a gang of hermaphrodite gunslingers take refuge from a demon plague in Telos: a town where its citizens have televisions instead of heads. **184 pages $12**

BB-027 "Siren Promised" Jeremy Robert Johnson & Alan M Clark
- Nominated for the Bram Stoker Award. A potent mix of bad drugs, bad dreams, brutal bad guys, and surreal/incredible art by Alan M. Clark. **190 pages $13**

BB-030 "Grape City" Kevin L. Donihe - More Donihe-style comedic bizarro
about a demon named Charles who is forced to work a minimum wage job on Earth after Hell goes out of business. **108 pages $10**

BB-031"Sea of the Patchwork Cats" Carlton Mellick III - A quiet
dreamlike tale set in the ashes of the human race. For Mellick enthusiasts who also adore The Twilight Zone. **112 pages $10**

BB-032 "Extinction Journals" Jeremy Robert Johnson - An uncanny
voyage across a newly nuclear America where one man must confront the problems associated with loneliness, insane dieties, radiation, love, and an ever-evolving cockroach suit with a mind of its own. **104 pages $10**

BB-034 "The Greatest Fucking Moment in Sports" Kevin L. Donihe
- In the tradition of the surreal anti-sitcom Get A Life comes a tale of triumph and agape love from the master of comedic bizarro. **108 pages $10**

BB-035 "The Troublesome Amputee" John Edward Lawson - Disturb-
ing verse from a man who truly believes nothing is sacred and intends to prove it. **104 pages $9**

BB-037 "The Haunted Vagina" Carlton Mellick III - It's difficult to love a
woman whose vagina is a gateway to the world of the dead. **132 pages $10**

BB-042 "Teeth and Tongue Landscape" Carlton Mellick III - On a
planet made out of meat, a socially-obsessive monophobic man tries to find his place amongst the strange creatures and communities that he comes across. **110 pages $10**

BB-043 **"War Slut" Carlton Mellick III** - Part "1984," part "Waiting for Godot," and part action horror video game adaptation of John Carpenter's "The Thing." **116 pages $10**

BB-045 **"Dr. Identity" D. Harlan Wilson** - Follow the Dystopian Duo on a killing spree of epic proportions through the irreal postcapitalist city of Bliptown where time ticks sideways, artificial Bug-Eyed Monsters punish citizens for consumer-capitalist lethargy, and ultraviolence is as essential as a daily multivitamin. **208 pages $15**

BB-047 **"Sausagey Santa" Carlton Mellick III** - A bizarro Christmas tale featuring Santa as a piratey mutant with a body made of sausages. 124 pages $10

BB-048 **"Misadventures in a Thumbnail Universe" Vincent Sakowski** - Dive deep into the surreal and satirical realms of neo-classical Blender Fiction, filled with television shoes and flesh-filled skies. **120 pages $10**

BB-049 **"Vacation" Jeremy C. Shipp** - Blueblood Bernard Johnson leaved his boring life behind to go on The Vacation, a year-long corporate sponsored odyssey. But instead of seeing the world, Bernard is captured by terrorists, becomes a key figure in secret drug wars, and, worse, doesn't once miss his secure American Dream. **160 pages $14**

BB-053 **"Ballad of a Slow Poisoner" Andrew Goldfarb** Millford Mutterwurst sat down on a Tuesday to take his afternoon tea, and made the unpleasant discovery that his elbows were becoming flatter. **128 pages $10**

BB-055 **"Help! A Bear is Eating Me" Mykle Hansen** - The bizarro, heartwarming, magical tale of poor planning, hubris and severe blood loss...
150 pages $11

BB-056 **"Piecemeal June" Jordan Krall** - A man falls in love with a living sex doll, but with love comes danger when her creator comes after her with crab-squid assassins. **90 pages $9**

BB-058 **"The Overwhelming Urge" Andersen Prunty** - A collection of bizarro tales by Andersen Prunty. **150 pages $11**

BB-059 **"Adolf in Wonderland" Carlton Mellick III** - A dreamlike adventure that takes a young descendant of Adolf Hitler's design and sends him down the rabbit hole into a world of imperfection and disorder. **180 pages $11**

BB-061 **"Ultra Fuckers" Carlton Mellick III** - Absurdist suburban horror about a couple who enter an upper middle class gated community but can't find their way out. **108 pages $9**

BB-062 **"House of Houses" Kevin L. Donihe** - An odd man wants to marry his house. Unfortunately, all of the houses in the world collapse at the same time in the Great House Holocaust. Now he must travel to House Heaven to find his departed fiancee. **172 pages $11**

BB-064 **"Squid Pulp Blues" Jordan Krall** - In these three bizarro-noir novellas, the reader is thrown into a world of murderers, drugs made from squid parts, deformed gun-toting veterans, and a mischievous apocalyptic donkey. **204 pages $12**

BB-065 **"Jack and Mr. Grin" Andersen Prunty** - "When Mr. Grin calls you can hear a smile in his voice. Not a warm and friendly smile, but the kind that seizes your spine in fear. You don't need to pay your phone bill to hear it. That smile is in every line of Prunty's prose." - Tom Bradley. **208 pages $12**

BB-066 **"Cybernetrix" Carlton Mellick III** - What would you do if your normal everyday world was slowly mutating into the video game world from Tron? **212 pages $12**

BB-072 **"Zerostrata" Andersen Prunty** - Hansel Nothing lives in a tree house, suffers from memory loss, has a very eccentric family, and falls in love with a woman who runs naked through the woods every night. **144 pages $11**

BB-073 **"The Egg Man" Carlton Mellick III** - It is a world where humans reproduce like insects. Children are the property of corporations, and having an enormous ten-foot brain implanted into your skull is a grotesque sexual fetish. Mellick's industrial urban dystopia is one of his darkest and grittiest to date. **184 pages $11**

BB-074 **"Shark Hunting in Paradise Garden" Cameron Pierce** - A group of strange humanoid religious fanatics travel back in time to the Garden of Eden to discover it is invested with hundreds of giant flying maneating sharks. **150 pages $10**

BB-075 **"Apeshit" Carlton Mellick III** - Friday the 13th meets Visitor Q. Six hipster teens go to a cabin in the woods inhabited by a deformed killer. An incredibly fucked-up parody of B-horror movies with a bizarro slant. **192 pages $12**

BB-076 **"Fuckers of Everything on the Crazy Shitting Planet of the Vomit At smosphere" Mykle Hansen** - Three bizarro satires. Monster Cocks, Journey to the Center of Agnes Cuddlebottom, and Crazy Shitting Planet. **228 pages $12**

BB-077 **"The Kissing Bug" Daniel Scott Buck** - In the tradition of Roald Dahl, Tim Burton, and Edward Gorey, comes this bizarro anti-war children's story about a bohemian conenose kissing bug who falls in love with a human woman. **116 pages $10**

BB-078 **"MachoPoni" Lotus Rose** - It's My Little Pony... *Bizarro* style! A long time ago Poniworld was split in two. On one side of the Jagged Line is the Pastel Kingdom, a magical land of music, parties, and positivity. On the other side of the Jagged Line is Dark Kingdom inhabited by an army of undead ponies. **148 pages $11**

BB-079 **"The Faggiest Vampire" Carlton Mellick III** - A Roald Dahl-esque children's story about two faggy vampires who partake in a mustache competition to find out which one is truly the faggiest. **104 pages $10**

BB-080 **"Sky Tongues" Gina Ranalli** - The autobiography of Sky Tongues, the biracial hermaphrodite actress with tongues for fingers. Follow her strange life story as she rises from freak to fame. **204 pages $12**

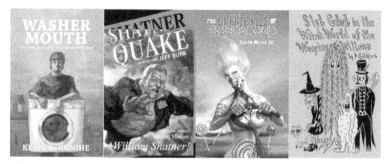

BB-081 **"Washer Mouth" Kevin L. Donihe** - A washing machine becomes human and pursues his dream of meeting his favorite soap opera star. **244 pages $11**

BB-082 **"Shatnerquake" Jeff Burk** - All of the characters ever played by William Shatner are suddenly sucked into our world. Their mission: hunt down and destroy the real William Shatner. **100 pages $10**

BB-083 **"The Cannibals of Candyland" Carlton Mellick III** - There exists a race of cannibals that are made of candy. They live in an underground world made out of candy. One man has dedicated his life to killing them all. **170 pages $11**

BB-084 **"Slub Glub in the Weird World of the Weeping Willows"** **Andrew Goldfarb** - The charming tale of a blue glob named Slub Glub who helps the weeping willows whose tears are flooding the earth. There are also hyenas, ghosts, and a voodoo priest **100 pages $10**

BB-085 **"Super Fetus" Adam Pepper** - Try to abort this fetus and he'll kick your ass! **104 pages $10**

BB-086 **"Fistful of Feet" Jordan Krall** - A bizarro tribute to spaghetti westerns, featuring Cthulhu-worshipping Indians, a woman with four feet, a crazed gunman who is obsessed with sucking on candy, Syphilis-ridden mutants, sexually transmitted tattoos, and a house devoted to the freakiest fetishes. **228 pages $12**

BB-087 **"Ass Goblins of Auschwitz" Cameron Pierce** - It's Monty Python meets Nazi exploitation in a surreal nightmare as can only be imagined by Bizarro author Cameron Pierce. **104 pages $10**

BB-088 **"Silent Weapons for Quiet Wars" Cody Goodfellow** - "This is high-end psychological surrealist horror meets bottom-feeding low-life crime in a techno-thrilling science fiction world full of Lovecraft and magic..." -John Skipp **212 pages $12**

BB-089 "Warrior Wolf Women of the Wasteland" Carlton Mellick III
Road Warrior Werewolves versus McDonaldland Mutants...post-apocalyptic fiction has never been quite like this. **316 pages $13**

BB-090 "Cursed" Jeremy C Shipp - The story of a group of characters who believe they are cursed and attempt to figure out who cursed them and why. A tale of stylish absurdism and suspenseful horror. **218 pages $15**

BB-091 "Super Giant Monster Time" Jeff Burk - A tribute to choose your own adventures and Godzilla movies. Will you escape the giant monsters that are rampaging the fuck out of your city and shit? Or will you join the mob of alien-controlled punk rockers causing chaos in the streets? What happens next depends on you. **188 pages $12**

BB-092 "Perfect Union" Cody Goodfellow - "Cronenberg's THE FLY on a grand scale: human/insect gene-spliced body horror, where the human hive politics are as shocking as the gore." -John Skipp. **272 pages $13**

BB-093 "Sunset with a Beard" Carlton Mellick III - 14 stories of surreal science fiction. **200 pages $12**

BB-094 "My Fake War" Andersen Prunty - The absurd tale of an unlikely soldier forced to fight a war that, quite possibly, does not exist. It's Rambo meets Waiting for Godot in this subversive satire of American values and the scope of the human imagination. **128 pages $11**

BB-095 "Lost in Cat Brain Land" Cameron Pierce - Sad stories from a surreal world. A fascist mustache, the ghost of Franz Kafka, a desert inside a dead cat. Primordial entities mourn the death of their child. The desperate serve tea to mysterious creatures.
A hopeless romantic falls in love with a pterodactyl. And much more. **152 pages $11**

BB-096 "The Kobold Wizard's Dildo of Enlightenment +2" Carlton Mellick III - A Dungeons and Dragons parody about a group of people who learn they are only made up characters in an AD&D campaign and must find a way to resist their nerdy teenaged players and retarded dungeon master in order to survive. 232 **pages $12**

BB-097 "My Heart Said No, but the Camera Crew Said Yes!" Bradley Sands - A collection of short stories that are crammed with the delightfully odd and the scurrilously silly. **140 pages $13**

BB-098 "A Hundred Horrible Sorrows of Ogner Stump" Andrew Goldfarb - Goldfarb's acclaimed comic series. A magical and weird journey into the horrors of everyday life. **164 pages $11**

BB-099 "Pickled Apocalypse of Pancake Island" Cameron Pierce A demented fairy tale about a pickle, a pancake, and the apocalypse. **102 pages $8**

BB-100 "Slag Attack" Andersen Prunty - Slag Attack features four visceral, noir stories about the living, crawling apocalypse. A slag is what survivors are calling the slug-like maggots raining from the sky, burrowing inside people, and hollowing out their flesh and their sanity. **148 pages $11**

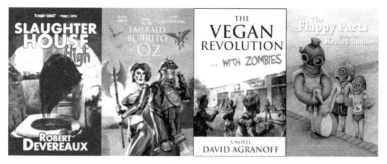

BB-101 "Slaughterhouse High" Robert Devereaux - A place where schools are built with secret passageways, rebellious teens get zippers installed in their mouths and genitals, and once a year, on that special night, one couple is slaughtered and the bits of their bodies are kept as souvenirs. **304 pages $13**

BB-102 "The Emerald Burrito of Oz" John Skipp & Marc Levinthal OZ IS REAL! Magic is real! The gate is really in Kansas! And America is finally allowing Earth tourists to visit this weird-ass, mysterious land. But when Gene of Los Angeles heads off for summer vacation in the Emerald City, little does he know that a war is brewing...a war that could destroy both worlds. **280 pages $13**

BB-103 "The Vegan Revolution... with Zombies" David Agranoff When there's no more meat in hell, the vegans will walk the earth. **160 pages $11**

BB-104 "The Flappy Parts" Kevin L Donihe - Poems about bunnies, LSD, and police abuse. You know, things that matter. 132 **pages $11**

BB-105 **"Sorry I Ruined Your Orgy" Bradley Sands** - Bizarro humorist Bradley Sands returns with one of the strangest, most hilarious collections of the year. **130 pages $11**

BB-106 **"Mr. Magic Realism" Bruce Taylor** - Like Golden Age science fiction comics written by Freud, *Mr. Magic Realism* is a strange, insightful adventure that spans the furthest reaches of the galaxy, exploring the hidden caverns in the hearts and minds of men, women, aliens, and biomechanical cats. **152 pages $11**

BB-107 **"Zombies and Shit" Carlton Mellick III** - "Battle Royale" meets "Return of the Living Dead." Mellick's bizarro tribute to the zombie genre. **308 pages $13**

BB-108 **"The Cannibal's Guide to Ethical Living" Mykle Hansen** - Over a five star French meal of fine wine, organic vegetables and human flesh, a lunatic delivers a witty, chilling, disturbingly sane argument in favor of eating the rich.. **184 pages $11**

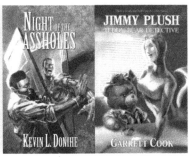

BB-109 **"Starfish Girl" Athena Villaverde** - In a post-apocalyptic underwater dome society, a girl with a starfish growing from her head and an assassin with sea anenome hair are on the run from a gang of mutant fish men. **160 pages $11**

BB-110 **"Lick Your Neighbor" Chris Genoa** - Mutant ninjas, a talking whale, kung fu masters, maniacal pilgrims, and an alcoholic clown populate Chris Genoa's surreal, darkly comical and unnerving reimagining of the first Thanksgiving. **303 pages $13**

BB-111 **"Night of the Assholes" Kevin L. Donihe** - A plague of assholes is infecting the countryside. Normal everyday people are transforming into jerks, snobs, dicks, and douchebags. And they all have only one purpose: to make your life a living hell.. **192 pages $11**

BB-112 **"Jimmy Plush, Teddy Bear Detective" Garrett Cook** - Hardboiled cases of a private detective trapped within a teddy bear body. **180 pages $11**

CPSIA information can be obtained
at www.ICGtesting.com
Printed in the USA
BVHW071038150620
581516BV00002B/65